Lerner SPORTS

GREATEST OF ALL TIME PLAYERS

G.O.A.T. FOOTBALL OFFENSIVE LINEMEN

Audrey Stewart

Lerner Publications ◆ Minneapolis

Lerner Publications Company
An imprint of Lerner Publishing Group, Inc.
241 First Avenue North
Minneapolis, MN 55401 USA

For reading levels and more information, look up this title at www.lernerbooks.com.

Main body text set in Aptifer Sans LT Pro.
Typeface provided by Linotype AG.

Library of Congress Cataloging-in-Publication Data

Names: Stewart, Audrey, author.
Title: G.O.A.T. football offensive linemen / Audrey Stewart.
Other titles: Greatest of all time football offensive linemen
Description: Minneapolis, MN : Lerner Publications, [2025] | Series: Lerner sports. Greatest of all time players | Includes bibliographical references and index. | Audience: Ages 7–11 | Audience: Grades 2–3 | Summary: "The best football offensive lineman can control the line of scrimmage, protect their quarterback, and open lanes for running backs. Meet the biggest, toughest players in the NFL. Compare their careers and choose your winners!"—Provided by publisher.
Identifiers: LCCN 2023049825 (print) | LCCN 2023049826 (ebook) | ISBN 9798765625842 (library binding) | ISBN 9798765628805 (paperback) | ISBN 9798765633885 (epub)
Subjects: LCSH: Football players—United States—Biography—Juvenile literature. | Football players—Rating of—United States—Juvenile literature. | Football—Offense—Juvenile literature.
Classification: LCC GV939.A1 S749 2025 (print) | LCC GV939.A1 (ebook) | DDC 796.332092/2—dc23/eng/20231122

LC record available at https://lccn.loc.gov/2023049825
LC ebook record available at https://lccn.loc.gov/2023049826

Manufactured in the United States of America
1 - CG - 7/15/24

TABLE OF CONTENTS

Offensive lineman Trent Williams (*right*) blocks a Las Vegas Raiders defender to protect his quarterback.

THE BLOCKERS

The San Francisco 49ers were playing the Las Vegas Raiders in January 2023. Offensive lineman Trent Williams was a force for the 49ers. His blocking from the left side of the offensive line allowed 49ers quarterback Brock Purdy to pass to wide receiver Brandon Aiyuk in the first quarter. Aiyuk scored San Francisco's first touchdown and tied the game 7–7.

FACTS AT A GLANCE

- » **JOHN HANNAH** WON THE OFFENSIVE LINEMAN OF THE YEAR AWARD FOR FOUR STRAIGHT YEARS IN 1978, 1979, 1980, AND 1981.
- » **MIKE WEBSTER'S** 220 GAMES PLAYED ARE THE SECOND MOST IN PITTSBURGH STEELERS HISTORY.
- » **BRUCE MATTHEWS** PLAYED 19 NATIONAL FOOTBALL LEAGUE (NFL) SEASONS. HE PLAYED EVERY POSITION ON THE OFFENSIVE LINE.
- » **TRENT WILLIAMS** WAS PICKED TO PLAY IN THE PRO BOWL 10 YEARS IN A ROW FROM 2012 TO 2022.

The game was tied 24–24 early in the fourth quarter. The 49ers and the Raiders each scored 10 points, and the game went into overtime tied 34–34. Thanks largely to Williams, the Las Vegas defenders could not get to Purdy. The quarterback could take his time throwing the ball. Williams's great blocking helped the 49ers win 37–34. Purdy had 22 completed passes for 284 yards and two touchdowns.

Trent Williams

The offensive line is made up of five players who begin each play at the line of scrimmage. Their job is to block the other team's defense to keep their quarterback safe. Offensive linemen also block to open running lanes for running backs.

Offensive linemen include offensive guards, offensive tackles, and centers. Centers are in the middle of the offensive line. They snap the ball to the quarterback at the start of a play. Guards line up on both sides of the center. Tackles are the players on the ends of the offensive line.

Nicknamed Iron Mike for his strength as a player and leader, Mike Webster (*right*) played most of his career with the Pittsburgh Steelers.

In 2002, the Tennessee Titans retired the number 74 to honor Bruce Matthews. That means no other player on the team can wear the number.

Offensive linemen are key to a team's ability to run and pass the ball. When offensive linemen don't do their jobs correctly, their quarterbacks get sacked and their running backs have nowhere to run. The best offensive linemen protect their teammates and help their teams win.

NO. 10 TRENT WILLIAMS

The Washington Redskins picked tackle Trent Williams in the 2010 NFL Draft. He played in the Pro Bowl every year from 2012 to 2018 while he was with Washington. Williams joined the San Francisco 49ers for the 2020 season.

Williams has amazing strength and skill. He is also fast for a player of his size. At 6 feet 5 (2 m) and 320 pounds (145 kg), he is a great pass and run blocker. During the 2022 season, Williams led San Francisco's offensive line and protected the team's quarterbacks. He didn't allow a sack in 17 games. Rookie quarterback Brock Purdy played the last nine games of the season and threw for 1,374 passing yards and 13 touchdowns. The team finished the regular season with a 13–4 record. Williams and the 49ers' offensive line helped Purdy succeed.

Each season, NFL Network makes a list of the league's top 100 players. Williams has made the list eight times. In 2023, he was number 14, the highest-ever ranking for an offensive lineman.

TRENT WILLIAMS STATS

Regular-Season Games Started	177
Pro Bowls	11
First-Team All-Pro	3 times
Top 100 Players List	8 times

Stats are accurate through the 2023 NFL season.

NO. 9 MIKE WEBSTER

Mike Webster joined the Pittsburgh Steelers for the 1974 season. He played in 14 games that year. Playing as a center, Webster was an All-Rookie player and helped the team achieve a 10–3–1 regular-season record. Webster and the Steelers won the 1975 Super Bowl with quarterback Terry Bradshaw.

Over the next 10 seasons, Webster and the Pittsburgh offensive line played a huge part in Bradshaw's 27,989 passing yards. Without a strong offensive line, Steelers running back Franco Harris wouldn't have been able to rush for 1,000 yards six seasons in a row. Webster's blocking led to Harris's success.

Webster played in six American Football Conference (AFC) championship games with Pittsburgh. After winning the Super Bowl in 1975, he won it three more times with the team in 1976, 1979, and 1980. Webster played 15 seasons with the Steelers. Only Ben Roethlisberger played more seasons on the team, with 18.

MIKE WEBSTER STATS

Regular-Season Games Started	217
Pro Bowls	9
First-Team All-Pro	5 times
Top 100 Players List	4 times

NO. 8 JASON KELCE

Jason Kelce joined the Philadelphia Eagles in 2011. The center is quick and knows how to block strong NFL defenders. He became a Pro Bowl player in 2014, his fourth year in the NFL.

In 2017, Kelce and the Eagles went 13–3 and reached the 2018 Super Bowl against the New England Patriots. Kelce helped the Eagles run a trick play with 34 seconds left in the second quarter. The Eagles were trying to score from the 1-yard line. Instead of lining up behind Kelce, quarterback

Nick Foles moved to the side of the offensive line. Kelce snapped the ball to running back Corey Clement. Clement pitched it to teammate Trey Burton. Kelce blocked Patriots defenders as Burton threw the ball to Foles. Foles was wide open when he caught the ball in the end zone for a touchdown. Kelce and Philadelphia won the game 41–33.

In 2022, Kelce and the Eagles had another great season. They went 14–3 and reached the Super Bowl again. But this time they lost to the Kansas City Chiefs 38–35. In 2023, Kelce was named to the NFL Top 100 Players list for the fifth time.

JASON KELCE STATS

Playoff Games Started	12
Pro Bowls	7
First-Team All-Pro	6 times
Super Bowl Wins	1

Stats are accurate through the 2023 NFL season.

NO. 7 JOHN HANNAH

John Hannah played guard for the Patriots from 1973 to 1985. Hannah won the Offensive Lineman of the Year award four straight years in 1978, 1979, 1980, and 1981. He was a First-Team All-Pro player seven times.

Two seasons stand out for Hannah and the Patriots. In 1976, fans saw one of the most talented Patriots teams in history.

They finished the regular season with a record of 11–3. The team had 2,948 total rushing yards thanks largely to Hannah and the offensive line. This was the fifth most in NFL history at the time. Hannah was a First-Team All-Pro player that season.

In 1978, Hannah and the offensive line helped New England rush for 3,165 yards, the second most in NFL history. Four different players ran for more than 500 yards, including quarterback Steve Grogan. In 1991, Hannah became the first player from the Patriots to join the Pro Football Hall of Fame.

JOHN HANNAH STATS

Regular-Season Games Started	183
Pro Bowls	9
First-Team All-Pro	7 times
Touchdowns	1

NO. 6 RANDALL MCDANIEL

Randall McDaniel started his NFL career in 1988 as a guard with the Minnesota Vikings. He played in the Pro Bowl every year except two until he retired from playing in 2001. During his career, McDaniel blocked for six different players who rushed for at least 1,000 yards in a season. He also blocked for five different players who had at least 3,000 passing yards.

McDaniel helped the 1998 Vikings go 15–1 in the regular season. They were the third team in NFL history to win 15 games. McDaniel and the Vikings set a record at the time by scoring 556 points.

As a guard, McDaniel was skilled at pass blocking. He helped the quarterback do his job. He allowed only 1.5 sacks in the 1998 season. McDaniel was also a great run blocker. He helped create space for the ballcarrier to run and gain yards. Running backs averaged 5.4 yards per carry with McDaniel on the offensive line. He joined the Pro Football Hall of Fame in 2009.

RANDALL MCDANIEL STATS

Regular-Season Games Started	220
Playoff Games Started	15
Pro Bowls	12
First-Team All-Pro	7 times

NO. 5 WILLIE ROAF

The New Orleans Saints picked Willie Roaf in the first round of the 1993 NFL Draft. He played tackle. At 6 feet 5 (2 m) and 320 pounds (145 kg), he wasn't easy for defenders to beat. In his second season, he was a

First-Team All-Pro player. He also played in his first of 11 Pro Bowl games. When he retired, Roaf had played in more Pro Bowls than any other Saints player in history.

One of Roaf's best seasons with the Saints was in 2000. He played in all 16 regular-season games. He helped the team reach a 10–6 record. In the playoffs, New Orleans faced the St. Louis Rams, the defending Super Bowl champions. With Roaf blocking, Saints quarterback Aaron Brooks completed 16 passes for 266 yards. The Saints won 31–28. Roaf was one of the best Saints players of all time.

WILLIE ROAF STATS

Regular-Season Games Started	189
Playoff Games Started	3
Pro Bowls	11
First-Team All-Pro	4 times

NO. 4

JONATHAN OGDEN

Jonathan Ogden was an NFL tackle and guard from 1996 to 2007. He played his entire career with the Baltimore Ravens. He was a Pro Bowl player in 11 of his 12 NFL seasons.

One of Ogden's best seasons was in 2000. His blocking created space for his teammates to succeed. Running backs Jamal Lewis and Priest Holmes had a combined 1,952 rushing yards and 59 catches. The Ravens finished the season 12–4 and advanced to their first Super Bowl. Baltimore defeated the New York Giants 34–7.

Ogden continued to show his skill as a pass protector and a run blocker. He won the 2002 Offensive Lineman of the Year award. In 2003, Ogden helped running back Jamal Lewis rush for 2,066 yards. This total ranks third in NFL history. Ogden retired from playing in 2008 and joined the Pro Football Hall of Fame in 2013.

JONATHAN OGDEN STATS

Regular-Season Games Started	176
Touchdowns	2
Pro Bowls	11
First-Team All-Pro	4 times

NO. 3

LARRY ALLEN

Larry Allen played tackle and guard for the Dallas Cowboys from 1994 to 2006. He was part of the offensive line that helped Dallas become one of the best teams of the 1990s. In his second season, Allen helped running back Emmitt Smith set a then Cowboys season record of 1,773 rushing yards.

The Cowboys finished third in total yards gained that season, and Allen played in his first Pro Bowl.

The Cowboys went 12–4 in 1995. Allen's strength and skill helped the team reach the Super Bowl in January 1996. With Allen blocking for Smith and quarterback Troy Aikman, the Cowboys beat the Steelers 27–17. In 1996 and 1997, Allen won the NFC Offensive Lineman of the Year award. He joined the Pro Football Hall of Fame in 2013.

LARRY ALLEN STATS

Regular-Season Games Started	197
Playoff Games Started	10
Pro Bowls	11
First-Team All-Pro	6 times

NO. 2 BRUCE MATTHEWS

Bruce Matthews played guard, tackle, and center from 1983 to 2001. He spent his entire 19-season NFL career with the Houston Oilers. In 1997, the Oilers moved to Memphis, Tennessee. They became the Tennessee Titans. Matthews played every position on Tennessee's offensive line. Playing different positions made him a smarter player.

In 1991, the Oilers won their first division title in 25 years. Matthews led the team to a great season in 1993. They lost four of their first five games, but they won the next 11 to finish the regular season 12–4. It was the team's best record yet.

Matthews played six of his last seven NFL seasons at guard. He started in 15 career playoff games and won the Offensive Lineman of the Year award three times. Matthews ranks first in the NFL for most career starts with one team at 293. He never missed a game because of an injury, and he ranks third on the NFL all-time leaderboard with 293 games started.

BRUCE MATTHEWS STATS

Regular-Season Games Started	293
Playoff Games Started	15
Pro Bowls	14
First-Team All-Pro	7 times

NO. 1 ANTHONY MUÑOZ

Few offensive linemen can match the skills of Anthony Muñoz. Muñoz joined the Cincinnati Bengals in 1980. He played tackle for 13 seasons in Cincinnati. His strength, speed, and balance earned him the Offensive Lineman of the Year award in 1981, 1987, and 1988. He played in the Pro Bowl in 11 of his 13 seasons.

Muñoz was a starting player for the Bengals in his first season. He continued to play a major role in the team's offensive line throughout his career. He rarely missed a game in his first 12 seasons. Muñoz was faster than most linemen. And at 6 feet 6 (2 m) and 278 pounds (126 kg), he was a huge presence on the field. He was skilled at blocking defenders and protecting quarterbacks and running backs. Muñoz could also catch the ball. He had seven career catches and four touchdowns for the Bengals. His wide range of skills made him the best offensive lineman of all time.

ANTHONY MUÑOZ STATS

Regular-Season Games Started	184
Touchdowns	4
Pro Bowls	11
First-Team All-Pro	9 times

EVEN MORE G.O.A.T.

There have been so many amazing offensive linemen in NFL history. Choosing only 10 is a challenge. Here are 10 others who could have made the G.O.A.T. list.

No. 11 WILL SHIELDS

No. 12 MIKE MUNCHAK

No. 13 ALAN FANECA

No. 14 JIM OTTO

No. 15 GENE UPSHAW

No. 16 DAVID BAKHTIARI

No. 17 QUENTON NELSON

No. 18 ZACH MARTIN

No. 19 DAN DIERDORF

No. 20 ORLANDO PACE

YOUR G.O.A.T.

It's your turn to make a G.O.A.T. list about offensive linemen. Start by doing research. Consider the rankings in this book. Then check out the Learn More section on page 31. Explore the books and websites to learn more about football players of the past and present.

You can search online for more information about great players too. Check with a librarian, who may have other resources for you. You might even try reaching out to football teams or players to see what they think.

Once you're ready, make your list of the greatest players of all time. Then ask people you know to make G.O.A.T. lists and compare them. Do you have players no one else listed? Are you missing anybody your friends think is important? Talk it over and try to convince them that your list is the G.O.A.T.!

GLOSSARY

block: to slow down or stop an opponent

draft: when teams take turns choosing new players

end zone: the area at each end of a football field where players score touchdowns

First-Team All-Pro: a team made up of each season's best NFL players

line of scrimmage: an imaginary line that marks the position of the ball at the start of each play

offensive line: the five players on offense who line up in front of the quarterback and block defenders

Pro Bowl: the NFL's all-star game

rookie: a first-year player

sack: to tackle the quarterback behind the line of scrimmage

snap: putting the football in play by quickly passing it between the legs to a teammate

LEARN MORE

A Beginner's Guide to American Football Positions
https://www.nike.com/a/football-positions

Bo, Mitchell. *The Super Bowl*. Mendota Heights, MN: Apex, 2023.

Football: Offensive Line
https://ducksters.com/sports/football/offensive_line.php

Lowe, Alexander. *G.O.A.T. Football Quarterbacks*. Minneapolis: Lerner Publications, 2023.

Lowe, Alexander. *G.O.A.T. Football Running Backs*. Minneapolis: Lerner Publications, 2023.

Offensive Line Positions in Football
https://footballadvantage.com/offensive-line-positions/

INDEX

PHOTO ACKNOWLEDGMENTS

Image credits: Chris Unger/Contributor/Getty Images, p.4; Gregory Shamus/Staff/Getty Images, p.5; George Gojkovich/Contributor/Getty Images, p.6; George Gojkovich/Contributor/Getty Images, p.7; Michael Owens/Contributor/Getty Images, p.8; Cooper Neill/Contributor/Getty Images, p.9; Focus On Sport/Contributor/Getty Images, p.10; George Gojkovich/Contributor/Getty Images, p.11; Perry Knotts/Contributor/Getty Images, p.12; Mitchell Leff/Contributor/Getty Images, p.13; George Gojkovich/Contributor/Getty Images, p.14; Focus On Sport/Contributor/Getty Images, p.15; Allen Kee/Contributor/Getty Images, p.16; Martin Morrow/Contributor/Getty Images, p.17; George Gojkovich/Contributor/Getty Images, p.18; George Rose/Stringer/Getty Images, p.19; George Gojkovich/Contributor/Getty Images, p.20; Mitchell Layton/Contributor/Getty Images, p.21; Sporting News Archive/Contributor/Getty Images, p.22; Peter Brouillet/Contributor/Getty Images, p.23; George Gojkovich/Contributor/Getty Images, p.24; George Gojkovich/Contributor/Getty Images, p.25; George Gojkovich/Contributor/Getty Images, p.26; Focus On Sport/Contributor/Getty Images, p.27

Cover: John Strohsacker/Contributor/Getty Images; Peter Brouillet/Contributor/Getty Images; George Gojkovich/Contributor/Getty Images